QUEEN
NOOR

AMERICAN-BORN QUEEN OF JORDAN

SPECIAL LIVES IN HISTORY THAT BECOME

Signature LIVES

QUEEN

NOOR

AMERICAN-BORN QUEEN OF JORDAN

by Lucia Raatma

Content Adviser: M. Şükrü Hanioğlu, Ph.D., Chair,
Department of Near Eastern Studies,
Princeton University

Reading Adviser: Susan Kesselring, M.A., Literacy
Educator, Rosemount–Apple Valley–Eagan
(Minnesota) School District

COMPASS POINT BOOKS MINNEAPOLIS, MINNESOTA

Compass Point Books
3109 West 50th Street, #115
Minneapolis, MN 55410

Visit Compass Point Books on the Internet at *www.compasspointbooks.com*
or e-mail your request to *custserv@compasspointbooks.com*

Editor: Julie Gassman
Page Production: Noumenon Creative
Photo Researcher: Marcie C. Spence
Cartographer: XNR Productions, Inc.
Library Consultant: Kathleen Baxter

Art Director: Jaime Martens
Creative Director: Keith Griffin
Editorial Director: Carol Jones
Managing Editor: Catherine Neitge

Library of Congress Cataloging-in-Publication Data
Raatma, Lucia.
  Queen Noor: American-born queen of Jordan / by Lucia Raatma.
      p. cm.—(Signature lives)
  Includes bibliographical references and index.
  ISBN 0-7565-1595-5 (hard cover)
  1. Noor, Queen, consort of Hussein, King of Jordan, 1951– Juvenile lit-
erature. 2. Kings and rulers—Biography—Juvenile literature. I. Title. II.
Series.
  DS154.52.N87R33 2005
  956.9504'4092—dc22   2005025214

Signature Lives

MODERN WORLD

From 1900 to the present day, humanity and the world have undergone major changes. New political ideas resulted in worldwide wars. Fascism and communism divided some countries, and democracy brought others together. Drastic shifts in theories and practice tested the standards of personal freedoms and religious conventions as well as science, technology, and industry. These changes have created a need for world policies and an understanding of international relations. The new mind-set of the modern world includes a focus on humanitarianism and the belief that a global economy has made the world a more connected place.

Table of Contents

1 THE FUTURE QUEEN

ɘᴄ᠗᠅᠐᠐

One spring day in 1978, American Lisa Halaby's life changed forever. She was working for her father in the Middle Eastern country of Jordan. At his request, she accompanied him to a meeting with Jordan's King Hussein bin Talal. She had met the king and his wife several times before, but since then, King Hussein had lost his wife in a helicopter crash. After the appointment with her father, King Hussein invited Lisa to have lunch at his palace the next day.

She was hesitant to go, but she could hardly refuse the king of her hosting nation. Once at the palace, she quickly grew comfortable with the king. He introduced her to three of his children, and he proudly showed off the Arabian horses in his stables.

Queen Noor and King Hussein as newlyweds in Amman, Jordan

Lisa impressed the king by being honest with him as she looked around his palace. She had a background in architecture, so she pointed out places where the structure needed work. She may have been nervous, but she felt it was important to tell him about the problems she saw. Because of his position, the king was used to having people try to please him and agree with him. This young woman's straightforward manner was a welcome change.

For the next three weeks, Lisa and King Hussein spent a great deal of time together. It was clear that they had a special connection. Before long, the king asked to speak to Lisa's father about their future. On June 15, 1978, after a two-month courtship, they were married. Suddenly, Lisa Halaby from the United States had become Queen Noor of Jordan. She was just 26, and the king was 43.

Was this a fairy tale? Far from it. The new queen quickly realized that she had many responsibilities, not the least of which was helping to raise King Hussein's eight children from

Lisa Halaby at a press conference held to announce her engagement to King Hussein

three previous marriages. In the years to come, the king and queen had four more children, and they had to face many challenges together. Their reign was not straight out of a storybook. Instead, they found themselves trying to peacefully lead their country amid the turmoil of the Middle East.

Queen Noor not only supported her husband, but she was also in charge of many organizations. In 1979, she served as chair of the country's National Committee for the Child. In this position, she helped create parks, start a children's literature project, and launch a program for immunizing the children of her country. That same year, she founded the Royal Endowment for Culture and Education, an organization that promotes the development of higher education, culture, and the arts in Jordan.

In 1985, she began an ambitious project: the creation of the Noor Al Hussein Foundation. This foundation supports community

> The Middle East is a region that extends from the eastern Mediterranean Sea to the Persian Gulf. Some of the land is part of Asia, and some of it is part of Africa. The region is home to several cultural and ethnic groups including the Persians, Arabs, Israelis, and Turks. This area of the world is rich in oil, and controlling the supply is important to nations all over the globe. The region is also the birthplace of the Jewish, Christian, and Muslim religions. Religion is a source of strength as well as conflict for the people of the Middle East. Over time, the region has experienced wars that are based on religious, cultural, and economic differences.

Queen Noor visits with a child at an event hosted by her foundation in 2000.

development, family health, education, women's business ventures, and other forms of enterprise. Through this foundation, she has helped the country of Jordan grow culturally and economically.

She once explained her goals in her position as queen:

I have long thought of myself as a builder of bridges between cultures. But when I look back on the connections I have been trying to make all my life, I find that may not be the best metaphor after all. A bridge connects only two things, with a gulf between them. As travel and technology erase the physical distances between us, we need to connect so much more. We need to weave a tapestry of our individual human experiences, each, with its own strengths, contributes to the strength and the beauty of the whole.

As an American woman who married the king of Jordan, Queen Noor had a wonderful opportunity to influence and improve the world. ॐ

2 CHILDHOOD AND CHANGES

⸙

Lisa Najeeb Halaby grew up thousands of miles away from the land of Jordan. She was born on August 23, 1951, in Washington, D.C. Her father's family was from Syria, a country in the Middle East. Halaby means "one from Aleppo," the second largest city in Syria. Her mother, Doris, had a Swedish background. So even as a young girl, Lisa appreciated the unique contributions that all kinds of people bring to the world. She had two younger siblings, a brother named Christian and a sister named Alexa.

Lisa's grandfather on the Halaby side, named Najeeb, left Syria as a young boy and moved with his family to Lebanon and then to New York. As an adult, he and his wife, Laura, founded Halaby Galleries, a successful import-export and interior decorating

Lisa's family moved often, following the career of her father Najeeb, who once served as the director of the Federal Aviation Administration.

15 ෴

firm. Laura was the daughter of a Texas rancher, and many people wondered about her marrying an exotic man from Syria. But he was proud of his heritage and was thrilled for his name to be carried on when he and Laura had a son in 1915.

Najeeb died when his son, also named Najeeb (Lisa's father), was only 12 years old. Laura was left to raise him alone. After selling Halaby Galleries, she was able to afford the finest schools for Najeeb. She remarried, but when that union ended after a few years, she devoted herself to her son.

As Najeeb grew up, he developed a passion for flying and exploring the world. Though he earned a law degree from Yale, his interests in aviation led him to become a test pilot for the Lockheed Corporation during World War II (1939–1945). He also tested planes while serving in the Navy. Soon after the war, Najeeb met his future wife, Doris, and they made a home in Washington, D.C.

When Lisa was only 2 years old, her father was offered a job in New York, and the family relocated. In his new position with Eastern Airlines, he learned about the airline industry. About three years later, a job change moved the family to Los Angeles.

Moving so often was difficult for Lisa because she was terribly shy. At one point, her mother even asked a psychologist for help because she could not understand why Lisa was so quiet. Her quiet nature was in sharp contrast to her father's adventurous one. She explains:

> *Part of this social awkwardness no doubt stems from a sense of inadequacy, rooted in considerable part in my relationship with my father. He sought perfection and never seemed satisfied. I felt I could never measure up ...*

Fortunately, Lisa grew to love California. She adored their home and enjoyed the warm, sunny weather. Her days were spent swimming and devouring books from their huge library.

But in 1961, Lisa's surroundings changed again. John F. Kennedy had recently been elected president of the United States, and he asked Najeeb Halaby to be the director of the Federal Aviation Administration (FAA). Although it was a great honor, Halaby initially turned down the job. However, Kennedy knew he was the right man and insisted that Halaby join his

President John F. Kennedy (1917–1963)

17

administration. Soon, the Halaby family was heading back to Washington, D.C.

Moving across the country again was hard for Lisa. She had trouble making friends, and she disliked the huge change that had been thrust upon her. But she had a privileged life. Like the daughters of other Kennedy administration members, she attended the National Cathedral School. In addition, Laura Halaby had moved to Virginia to be near her son, so Lisa often visited her grandmother's farm. There she went horseback riding and escaped from the pressures of school.

One day while riding a horse near her grandmother's home, Lisa came upon a group of migrant workers. These families labored on farms, moving from place to place, as crops were ready to be planted and harvested. It was a hard life. The families were very poor and worked for hours in the hot sun. Lisa was shocked by what she saw, and she realized how different her life was from theirs. From that moment, she became sympathetic to those who were less fortunate than she was.

In spite of the opportunities she had, Lisa could see that her father was struggling. He had been used to making a significant amount of money in business, and working for the government paid a lower salary. He soon found himself in debt and worrying about how to support his family.

Civil rights leader Martin Luther King Jr. led the 1963 March on Washington. Lisa was inspired by his famous "I Have a Dream" speech.

But even with these problems, Lisa gained a great deal by living in Washington, D.C., at this time. The Kennedy presidency was an era full of hope and change. During the 1960s, the United States was undergoing a difficult transformation. The civil rights movement was making America take a good look at itself and the racism that ran throughout its borders. Laws that discriminated against blacks were being questioned. Leaders like Martin Luther King Jr. were challenging people to stand up for themselves and for their rights.

Lisa knew a little bit about prejudice. Sometimes her classmates teased her about her foreign last

19

name. She knew that her father sometimes faced unfair treatment because of his Syrian background. Kennedy's ideals of equality and justice appealed to her in a personal way. Even as a young girl, she began to consider how the world worked, and she noticed how different groups got along with one another. The seeds of her future work were being planted.

Lisa respected President Kennedy, and she dreamed of one day joining the Peace Corps, a volunteer organization that Kennedy helped create. So she was deeply saddened on November 22, 1963, when the president was assassinated. As Vice President Lyndon B. Johnson was sworn in to take his place, the nation was in shock. And Lisa's life was

The New York American Journal *reported the shocking news of Kennedy's assassination.*

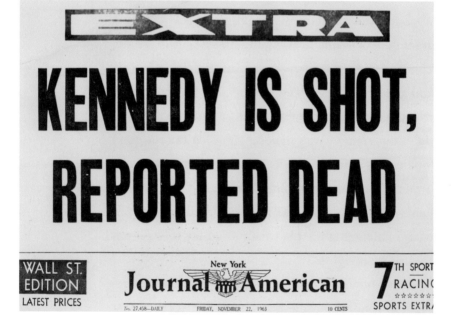

EXTRA

KENNEDY IS SHOT, REPORTED DEAD

WALL ST. EDITION
LATEST PRICES

New York
Journal American

No. 27,458—DAILY   FRIDAY, NOVEMBER 22, 1963   10 CENTS

7TH SPORT
RACING
★★★★★
SPORTS EXTRA

about to change again.

Najeeb Halaby stayed on with the FAA for a bit longer, but he finally found himself so far in debt that he had to resign and take a more profitable job. In 1965, Halaby accepted an offer with Pan American World Airways, and the family moved to New York again.

Once there, Lisa was enrolled at the Chapin School, which she loathed. The school discouraged discussions about social issues, an interest and passion of Lisa's. American soldiers were fighting in the Vietnam War. Protests were being held all over the country. But at Chapin, such matters were off-limits. Lisa begged her parents to let her leave and attend another school. Finally, they agreed. She finished high school at the Concord Academy, a school that praised academic achievement and self-discipline. Lisa loved the atmosphere there. She worked hard and immersed herself in her studies. Before long, her thoughts turned to college. ℘

3 FINDING HER WAY

Chapter

❧❧❧

Initially, Lisa Halaby planned to attend Stanford University, a well-respected school in California. The college had already accepted her for the fall of 1969, and she longed to return to the West Coast. However, Halaby had also been accepted at Princeton University in New Jersey. This school had long been an all-male institution, but that fall women would be allowed to attend for the first time. Intrigued by the chance to be part of its first coed class, Halaby chose Princeton.

Her transition to college was a hard one. She was one of very few women on campus—in fact, for every 22 men, there was only one woman. Then, after some upperclassmen teased her about her Arab background, Halaby felt like she didn't fit in.

When Princeton was founded in 1746, it was called the College of New Jersey and was located in the city of Elizabeth. Its first enrollment was just 10 young men. In 1756, the school moved to Princeton, New Jersey. In 1896, the name officially changed to Princeton University, and today more than 6,600 students study there. Princeton is a member of the Ivy League, a group of long-established and highly regarded Eastern U.S. colleges.

To make matters worse, during her first year at Princeton, her father was named CEO of Pan Am airline. This was an important position, so many students thought she was a wealthy snob.

As Halaby struggled with these personal challenges, the United States faced a global challenge. War in Vietnam continued. U.S. troops, trying to stop the spread of communism, battled alongside the South Vietnamese against communist North Vietnam. Many people were against U.S. involvement. Halaby voiced her own disapproval of the war and took part in student protests. At one point, police used tear gas on her and other protesters. Her experiences left her questioning the U.S. government and its actions.

At the same time, Halaby's mother was eager for her daughter to make her society debut in New York. Such parties introduced young women to society and announced their eligibility for marriage. Halaby remembers, "I found the whole idea absurd. … I sensed that she was being pressured by my

father's continuing need to be accepted." Halaby hated this tradition and felt this party was especially inappropriate in the climate of war. But to please her parents, she finally agreed to attend one debut party.

In the winter of 1971, Halaby decided to take some time off from college. She was unsure of her own goals, and she needed to get away from the pressures of her studies. She also needed time away from her family. So she moved to Colorado, where she worked as a waitress in a pizza parlor and a maid at a hotel. She also worked part time doing odd jobs at the Aspen Institute. While there, she helped on an architectural project and attended a thought-provoking conference

Halaby was shocked by events at Kent State University, where four students were killed in 1970 after the National Guard opened fire during a protest.

The Aspen Institute is an international nonprofit organization that is dedicated to promoting open communication and nurturing leadership through seminars, conferences, and leadership development programs. Members of the organization are involved in a wide variety of programs, ranging from education to health to philosophy and arts. The institute was founded in 1950 and is headquartered in Washington, D.C., with campuses in Aspen, Colorado, and on the Wye River in Maryland.

on "Technological Change and Social Responsibility."

Initially, her father was furious. He flew to Colorado and tried to convince her to go back to college. He could not understand why she needed to be on her own. But the time away from school helped her think about what was important to her, and her experiences at the Aspen Institute inspired her. When she returned to Princeton the next year, she declared a major in architecture and urban planning. She later observed that her studies in architecture "provided me with some very practical skills—a reduced need for sleep, and practice in thinking on my feet when faced with merciless critiques of my work. Both of these would prove very useful in later life."

When Halaby graduated from Princeton in 1974, she took a job with an architectural firm in Sydney, Australia, where she enjoyed exploring the country. After a year, she began working with Llewelyn-Davis, a planning company based in Great Britain. She was sent to work on a project in Tehran, the capital of

Iran. During her time in that city, she became very aware of the differences between the American and Middle Eastern cultures. She began to feel that the Middle East was misunderstood by Westerners.

Meanwhile, Najeeb Halaby had left Pan Am and become a consultant for Alia Airlines of Jordan. He also formed Arab Air Services, an aviation company that had an office in Amman, the capital of Jordan. Through this work, he and his wife had many opportunities to meet and socialize with King Hussein and his wife, Queen Alia. The king was a pilot and had a great interest in airplanes.

Queen Alia and King Hussein enjoyed a vacation in Switzerland. The queen was adored by the people of Jordan.

During her first visit to Jordan in 1976, Lisa enjoyed exploring the ancient ruins of the city of Petra.

In 1976, Lisa Halaby visited her father in Jordan and immediately fell in love with the Arab culture. It made her think about her own background. She was considering going back to school for her graduate degree in journalism, which she saw as a way to encourage understanding between the Middle Eastern and Western cultures. Meanwhile, she accepted another opportunity: to work for her father by filling in for an Arab Air Services manager who was ill.

It was during her first visit to Jordan in 1976 that Lisa Halaby first met King Hussein. He and his wife had attended a ceremony at the airport in Amman to celebrate Jordan's acquisition of the country's first Boeing 747 airplane. By chance that day, Lisa took a photograph of the king and her father, not realizing how important the king would become in her life less than two years later.

The more time Lisa spent in Jordan, the more attached she felt to the country. After her temporary job at Arab Air was over in mid-1977, she thought about journalism school at Columbia University, where she had been accepted. But she chose to stay in Jordan to work on planning and designing the offices for Royal Jordanian Airlines. She saw an opportunity to apply her architectural training in a "meaningful way, [and she] could not resist the challenge."

Lisa worked as an architect in Jordan for several months before her fateful private lunch with King Hussein in April 1978.

4 BECOMING QUEEN NOOR

഻ഀ

When King Hussein spoke with Najeeb Halaby and asked for his daughter's hand in marriage, Halaby was incredibly surprised. The proposal had come just a few weeks after Lisa visited the king's palace and offered her advice on structural problems. Najeeb knew the king and his daughter had met for lunch, but he had no idea that their relationship had become so serious in such a short time. Even Lisa Halaby had been shocked by the proposal. She remembers:

> *I agonized over my decision for the next two weeks, trying to work out in my mind whether I should question his judgment in considering me to be the right choice for him and for the country. Although none of his previous wives had been born in*

Jordan either, what might be the negative implications for him in the Arab world if he married me? Would it matter that I was born in the United States? Was I suitable? I had lived an independent life, traveled in many different countries. I had a free, open spirit. Would I have the self-discipline necessary to make a good wife for a king?

King Hussein was married three times before he married Lisa Halaby. The king was only 19 when he married his first wife Queen Dina in 1955. Their marriage lasted just 18 months. They had one daughter together. His second wife was Princess Muna. They were married from 1961 to 1972 and had four children. The same year he divorced Muna, Hussein married Queen Alia. The couple had two children together. They also adopted a daughter, Abir, a baby who had been orphaned when an airplane crashed into her home. Alia was killed in a helicopter crash in 1977.

Halaby also wondered about the three wives who had come before her. Was the king a playboy? Or could she trust him? But during those first weeks getting to know each other, Halaby had enjoyed long conversations, dinners, and movies with the king. Spending time with him was a joy, and she came to know the king as a man of high character. She realized that she was in love with him and wanted to be his wife. Her father was concerned because of their different backgrounds and because King Hussein would always be in danger as the leader of a troubled land. However, Najeeb ultimately supported his daughter's decision.

In a matter of days, Lisa Halaby's life was transformed. She never returned to her job. Suddenly, she was guarded by security at all times. She had to learn the difficult Arabic language. She chose to adopt Islam as her religion. And she gave up her American citizenship. These were huge changes for the independent woman.

Halaby also changed her name, as is common in conversions to the Islamic faith. King Hussein gave her what she called a gift when he named her Noor, which means "spiritual light of saintliness" in Arabic. Some say he chose that name because of her beautiful blonde hair. Others believe that she brought joy to his life after he had been widowed. As Noor Al Hussein, her name literally meant "light of Hussein."

The religion of Islam teaches that all faiths have one common message, which is the existence of a supreme being—a god known as Allah. By submitting and surrendering to God, one can live in peace. Islam is an Arabic word that means "submission to God." People who follow the Islamic faith are known as Muslims, and their most sacred book is the Koran. This book outlines the revelations given to the prophet Muhammad, whom Muslims consider to be a model for all people to follow.

Their wedding was small and private, nothing like royal weddings that people might watch on television. Guests included the king's mother, Queen Zein, and Noor's parents and siblings. The five-minute ceremony took place at Zahran Palace, Queen Zein's home. Noor wore a simple white dress and low-heeled shoes made especially for the event. Her hair was fixed simply, and she did not wear makeup. But Noor challenged tradition simply by attending the ceremony. According to Muslim tradition, the bride does not actually attend her own wedding. Instead, she is represented by a male relative. Some people respected her wishes, but others were critical of her choice to break from tradition.

The marriage ceremony took place in a beautifully furnished room with the couple, marriage official, and witnesses all seated.

For a honeymoon, the king and queen traveled to Scotland and England. Queen Noor longed to spend time with her new husband, but she soon learned that he had very little time to himself. His honeymoon

days were spent handling matters important to his country. And even when he could relax, he wanted to see his children, three of whom accompanied them on part of the honeymoon. Queen Noor had to accept that her husband was needed by many other people.

Once back from their trip, the king and queen lived in Hashimya Palace, the place where they had shared their first lunch together. But the palace's necessary renovations were noisy and inconvenient, so the royal family moved about. For some time, they lived in Al Nadwa Palace, a structure that was part offices and part living areas. They eventually settled into a new home that Noor helped design. It was called Bab al-Salam, which means "gate of peace."

All was not peaceful, however. Some Jordanians did not quickly accept Noor as their new queen. They were suspicious of her sudden conversion to Islam, and they perceived her to be a materialistic American who would never fit in. And it was a tense time for Jordan, a country that had long been plagued by tension between the Middle East and the West. ✍

Chapter

5 UNDERSTANDING JORDAN

ⲉⲟⲭⲟⲟ

Many of the challenges Noor faced as queen were deeply rooted in the history and politics of Jordan. The country lies in an area of the world known as the Middle East. This region has often been plagued by violence and unrest. The turmoil is in some part caused by the differing religions and cultures of the region. One subject of conflict is the status of Israel. This nation is comprised mostly of Jewish people, whose religious beliefs are different from those of the Muslims surrounding them.

The territory that makes up modern Jordan was the site of some of the earliest settlements in recorded history. Some of the regions east of the Jordan River, such as Edom, Gilead, and Moab, are often talked about in the Bible. Over the years, these

A painting from the mid-1800s of the ancient city of Petra, Jordan

kingdoms were conquered by groups such as the Egyptians, Assyrians, Babylonians, Persians, and Romans. In 636 A.D., the Arabs took Jordan from the Byzantine Empire, and it has been ruled by Muslim leaders ever since. From 1517 to 1918, Jordan was ruled by the Ottomans. The Ottomans had a vast empire—founded in the 13th century—that was centered in what is now Turkey. They controlled a huge area from the Balkan Peninsula to the Middle East and North Africa.

During World War I (1914–1918), the Ottomans opposed the Allied forces, including France, Great Britain, and others. Seeing a way to liberate Jordan from the Ottomans, King Hussein's great-grandfather, Sharif Hussein bin Ali, launched the Great Arab Revolt in 1916. He wanted to establish a unified kingdom for the Arab states, and he trusted Great Britain's promise to support such a kingdom. At the end of the war, the Ottomans had lost their power, but Britain did not honor its word to the Arabs. Instead, Great Britain and France established mandates in many former Arab provinces of the Ottoman empire.

Jordan and the land that is present-day Israel were awarded to Great Britain. In 1922, the British divided the area into two parts. The lands west of the Jordan River were named Palestine and those east of the river were Transjordan. Transjordan was placed under the rule of Abdullah ibn Hussein, King

Map shows boundaries of 1922.

Middle East, 1950

Borders of Jordan and surrounding areas saw significant change from the 1920s to 1950.

Hussein's grandfather. In February 1928, Transjordan obtained some independence in an agreement of autonomy with Great Britain.

During World War II (1939–1945), Transjordan served as a base of British operations. In 1945, Transjordan became a founding member of the Arab League, an organization that directed Arab

Formally known as the League of Arab States, the Arab League was formed in 1945 to provide a political voice for Arab nations. One purpose of the league was to improve the economies of its members. So it helped found the Arab Telecommunications Union, the Arab Postal Union, and the Arab Development Bank. The Arab Common Market, established in 1965, helps the Arab nations trade with one another. When the state of Israel was created in 1948, the league strongly opposed it. In recent years, the league has somewhat softened that position.

policy in international affairs. In March 1946, Transjordan became independent, no longer under British control. Abdullah ibn Hussein was named king.

In May 1948, the Transjordan army and other Arab League forces attacked the newly formed state of Israel. The army occupied sections of central Palestine, including the Old City of Jerusalem.

On April 24, 1950, despite strong opposition from other Arab League members, King Abdullah, whose views were considered somewhat pro-Western among Arab leaders, formally merged all of Arab-held Palestine with Transjordan and granted citizenship to West Bank residents. Then the prefix *trans* (across) no longer made sense, and the kingdom became known as the Hashemite Kingdom of Jordan. The word *Hashemite* refers to Hashim, the grandfather of the prophet Muhammad. All members of Jordanian royalty claim to be descended from him.

King Abdullah was assassinated on July 20, 1951,

Young King Hussein sits with his 2-year-old sister and 5-year-old brother on his coronation day.

by a Palestinian who feared he would sign a peace treaty with Israel. His son Talal then became king, but he had a mental illness and was removed from office the following year. On August 11, 1952, Talal's son Hussein II was named king. But Hussein was just 17, so a council ruled for him until May 2, 1953. On that day, his 18th birthday, King Hussein took the throne.

This was the man Queen Noor married. His history was the very history of Jordan. She did not take the responsibility lightly. ℘

6 RULING AMID CONFLICT

❧

When King Hussein accepted the throne in 1953, clashes between Jordan and Israel were already under way. One problem involved Israeli irrigation and hydroelectric plans that would have reduced the volume of the Jordan River, which creates part of the border between the two countries. The river's water was also vital to Jordanian development. Both countries accused one another of illegal raids and border violations. For decades, political, economic, and religious conflicts continued to plague these and other nations of the Middle East.

The Arab nations seemed to split into two groups. Syria, Egypt, and Iraq were part of an extremist group, while Jordan, Tunisia, and many small nations along the Persian Gulf were more

King Hussein visits a frontier army post during the Six-Day war in 1967.

In 1964, the Arab League created the Palestine Liberation Organization (PLO) as the official representative of the Palestinian people in the war against Israel. The PLO is an umbrella group made up of members of several organizations, including guerilla groups and associations of doctors, laborers, lawyers, students, teachers, and women. Over the years, the group has used terrorist methods to fight against Israel. Yet it maintains favorable relations with many countries and is recognized by the United Nations.

moderate. For a time, Jordan's border with Syria was as troubled as its border with Israel. Arab guerrilla fighters of the Palestine Liberation Organization (PLO) entered Jordan from Syria and launched terrorist attacks against Israel. The Israelis blamed Jordan for not preventing these attacks.

In July 1966, Jordan withdrew its support of the PLO. But in November, a massive Israeli raid killed 15 Jordanians and created intense pressure for King Hussein to once again back the PLO. When he refused, the PLO called for him to leave office, and clashes on the Syrian border increased.

While the future Queen Noor was arguing with her parents over which high school to attend, King Hussein was the leader of a nation facing war. In 1967, tensions between Israel and the Arab states increased and led to an armed conflict called the Six-Day War in June of that year. Israel defeated the military forces of Egypt, Syria, and Jordan, and gained control of the Sinai Peninsula, the Gaza Strip, the West Bank, and the

Golan Heights. These areas became known as the Occupied Territories.

In November 1967, the United Nations passed Resolution 242. This resolution called for Israel to withdraw from the Occupied Territories and for the Arab states to recognize Israel's independence and its legitimacy as a Jewish state. In spite of the United Nations passing the resolution, both Israel and the Arab states rejected it, and its terms were not followed.

In the years that followed, tensions between the Arab nations and Israel continued. But in September

Egyptian President Anwar Sadat (left) and Israeli Prime Minister Menachem Begin shake hands at the Camp David Accords as U.S. President Jimmy Carter looks on.

Anwar Sadat and Menachem Begin shared the 1978 Nobel Peace Prize for signing the Camp David peace agreement. Sadat was born in Egypt in 1918 as one of 13 children. When he was a young man, Egypt was controlled by the British Empire, and he was part of a revolutionary group that tried to overthrow that government. In 1970, years after Egypt gained its independence, Sadat became president of the country. Begin was born in White Russia, now known as Belarus, in 1913. He worked to bring about the establishment of the state of Israel in 1948, and he was elected prime minister of that state in 1977.

1978, just a few months after Queen Noor and King Hussein were wed, major progress was made in the peace process. The United States sponsored the Camp David Peace Accords. This agreement would return land that Israel had gained from Egypt, encourage trade between the two countries, and guarantee that neither Israel nor Egypt would attack the other. U.S. President Jimmy Carter was hailed as a hero for bringing Israeli Prime Minister Menachem Begin and Egyptian President Anwar Sadat together for this treaty.

King Hussein, however, did not support the effort. He felt that Jordan and the PLO should have been included in the discussion of peace in the Middle East. He also rejected the agreement because it did not call for Israeli withdrawal from all the Occupied Territories. When the accords were officially signed in March 1979, Carter asked for King Hussein's support, but he refused to give it. Many leaders in the United States could not understand the king's position, and they were disappointed when he would not stand behind the president.

While her husband was trying to be understood throughout the world, Queen Noor was trying to be understood in her adopted country. Many Jordanians did not trust her. When she tried to start programs that would help the women of Jordan, some people claimed she was too ambitious. Other people felt she cared only about jewelry and clothing and looking beautiful. In one instance, while the king was seeking aid from other Arab countries, the queen was seen in a jewelry store, and a newspaper in Kuwait ran this headline: "A king begs, a queen shops." The new queen had a long way to go in proving herself to the people of Jordan. ᴥ

7 BOTH MOTHER AND QUEEN

⌘

While ruling the country of Jordan was difficult and complicated, Queen Noor and King Hussein were thrilled with joyful news in 1979. The queen was pregnant. But the joy would soon be followed by sadness. While in England during her fifth month of pregnancy, she felt ill and eventually suffered a miscarriage. The king was busy in Baghdad, Iraq at the time, and Queen Noor told him to stay there. She endured the loss of their baby by herself.

In the months that followed, Queen Noor began to focus on her role in the nation of Jordan. She decided that her goals would include improving the country's health care system, taking care of its historical buildings, and bettering the lives of Jordan's women and children. She explained:

Queen Noor and King Hussein pose for photographers in their palace gardens in March 1984.

Child welfare and development was an urgent national priority because our population was so young: More than half of all Jordanians were under sixteen, and one-fifth were under five years old. Our birth rate was exceptionally high. ... [which] put immense pressure on all our services, particularly education and health. There was severe overcrowding in many schools ... an appalling shortage of children's books and very few facilities and parks, especially for children in poor neighborhoods.

In 1979, the queen was appointed chair of Jordan's National Committee for the Child. In this role, she created programs for immunizing children, building parks, promoting literacy, and establishing the country's first children's hospital. She also was concerned by the big gap between the rich and the poor in her country. She knew that one way to close that gap was by providing a good education for everyone. So that same year, she established the Royal Endowment for Culture and Education. This organization was the first to research the manpower needs of Jordan and provide scholarships in fields that could help the country's development.

Queen Noor knew that the Arab nations needed ways to be more unified. The Arab Children's Congress was one of her projects that tried to promote such unity. The congress allowed children

A girl marched with a flag to celebrate the United Nation's Year of the Child in 1979. Noor's work on the National Committee for the Child was part of this world-wide effort to improve conditions for children.

from across the Arab world to gather for two weeks and learn about one another through drama and art workshops. Though children from these nations all speak the same language, they face different problems and have different concerns. This project continues to encourage understanding throughout the Middle East.

In the midst of her work for children, Noor found out she was once again pregnant. She gave birth to Prince Hamzah on March 29, 1980. The king and queen were overjoyed, and Noor's stepchildren enjoyed having a new little brother to play with.

The baby traveled with the king and queen in June 1980, when they made their first visit to the United States since their wedding. Noor was excited to see her native country again, yet the visit was a difficult one. President Carter was still upset by King Hussein's comments about the Camp David Accords, so Noor's meetings with first lady Rosalynn Carter were rather tense. However, Queen Noor remained cordial and polite, determined to make the most of the meetings. She remembered in her autobiography that the young prince helped ease the tension when Rosalynn cooed over him and conversation turned to family and children.

While in the United States, the queen was discouraged by the American media. When interviewed, she wanted to talk about her husband's work and his commitment to peace. But reporters didn't listen to her ideas. Instead, they asked her about fashion and her romance with the king. In their minds, this tall, beautiful blonde was living a fairy tale. Those were the only details that interested them.

A year later, Queen Noor was asked to speak at the Center for Contemporary Arab Studies at

Georgetown University in Washington, D.C. She would be addressing professors and diplomats who knew a great deal about her country, so she was very nervous. But when the time came, she was able to relax. She succeeded in voicing her views about the Arab-Israeli conflict. She recalled, "The *Washington Post* sent a reporter from the Style section ... and once again, the resulting story focused as much on what I was wearing as on what I was saying, but at least I was quoted accurately on substance."

Queen Noor saw her speech at Georgetown as an opportunity to share her and the king's views on Middle Eastern policy.

On June 10, 1981, Queen Noor and King Hussein had another child, a boy they named Hashim. Two years later, on April 24, 1983, they had a little girl named Iman. This name means "faith" in Arabic. The queen indeed needed faith to survive those years. She had not planned to have another child so soon, and world events were proving tension-filled for the leaders of Jordan.

In 1980, Ronald Reagan had been elected president of the United States. His perspective on Israel was sympathetic and did not favor the Arab nations. Reagan tried to pressure King Hussein to sign a peace treaty with Israel, but Hussein felt he could not do so without the cooperation of Palestinians. However, neither the United States nor Israel would meet with the Palestinians until they accepted Israel's right to exist—a critical element of the U.N. Resolution 242.

The situation involving Palestinians, Israel, and Jordan was a complicated web of misunderstanding that Hussein tried to improve by meeting with Yasser Arafat, the leader of the PLO. When he was not successful in getting Arafat to recognize Resolution 242, the United States accused him of not helping the peace process. King Hussein and Queen Noor found this to be a frustrating and discouraging time.

Yasser Arafat was born in 1929 to a family of seven children. Growing up, he divided his time between Cairo, the capital of Egypt, and Jerusalem. After the Arab-Israeli War of 1948, Arafat began fighting for a Palestinian state. In 1969, he became chairman of the PLO. Over the years, there were many attempts on Arafat's life. He died in November 2004 after several years of poor health.

Yasser Arafat's full name is Mohammed Abdel-Raouf Arafat al-Qudwa al-Husseini. He was nicknamed Yasser, which means "easy-going," as a teenager.

On February 9, 1986, Queen Noor gave birth to her fourth child, a daughter named Raiyah, which means "flag" in Arabic. As she entered the world, her father continued his work for peace in the Middle East. For many years, he had suggested the idea of an international conference on Middle East peace. He felt negotiations that included countries throughout the world would be more effective and long-lasting than those that involved just two or three countries. While the United States and Israel were open to the idea of international negotiations, there was a problem. Israel would not recognize the PLO as the official representative of the Palestinian people, and the PLO continued to reject Resolution 242. It seemed to be an endless circle of interconnected problems. The queen remembered of her husband:

> *He always assumed he was negotiating with men of goodwill and that somehow, if he worked at it hard enough, he would be able to achieve peace and reconciliation. In this quest he was often beset by adversaries on every side. But he never, ever stopped trying.*

As the constant tension in the Middle East seemed to dominate the ruling of Jordan during the 1980s, Queen Noor had personal conflicts to deal with. For years, she had tried to be a good mother as well as a good queen, but it was always a challenge. At dinnertime and even story time, when she wanted to be completely devoted to her children, she was constantly interrupted with phone calls and emergencies.

She hated the idea of nannies raising her children, so she tried to be as hands-on as she could. She often wondered if her children were being cheated of "normal" childhoods. Yet she observed, "I like to think our children did have the advantage of growing up in an environment in which the concept of dedication to something larger than themselves was simply a part of life."

The children's lives were not without entertainment. In fact, many dignitaries from other countries liked to give animals as gifts to the royal family. At one time or another, their palace was home to horses, gazelles, chickens, dogs, rabbits, cats, guinea pigs, goats, and even a lion. One day, Queen Noor asked a nanny to bring her a camera, but the woman misunderstood. She was gone for some time and finally returned with a camel! The king and

Queen Noor looks like any average mother walking with her youngest child, Raiyah.

queen found this to be very funny, and the children enjoyed taking turns riding the camel all afternoon.

As the years passed and Queen Noor tried to juggle the day-to-day responsibilities of mothering her own small children, she also had to handle her adolescent stepchildren. Many children resent their stepmothers, and Noor's stepchildren were no exception. It did not help that their father was seldom present and therefore unable to bring harmony to the household.

At one point, the older children confronted their parents with a list of 54 complaints—some reasonable and some ridiculous. Noor was saddened by their actions and worried that she was more of a problem than a help. Feelings of helplessness and isolation lasted more than two years. She even wondered if her marriage could survive the conflicts with Hussein's children. But she drew strength from the respect she had for her husband.

> *I was able to get through these days by thinking about what Hussein himself had gone through: the many cruel betrayals and his forgiveness of them all, and the jealousy, attacks, and misunderstandings he had endured, his faith and humor intact. ... Because my husband always focused beyond himself on the greater good, I found myself trying to follow his example.*

Although her family life was proving to be a challenge, Queen Noor continued to focus some of her energy on national issues. One of her favorite projects was the Jerash Festival of Culture and Arts. The ancient city of Jerash was home to two well-preserved Roman theaters. Noor was inspired by the beautiful structures and suggested that "the magnificent ancient amphitheaters in Amman, Jerash, and Petra could provide superior venues for [cultural events]."

With the support of volunteers from Yarmouk University in Irbid, Noor launched the first festival

The love that the queen and king shared helped Queen Noor survive difficult times.

The National Egyptian Band performs in a theater of ancient ruins at the Jerash Festival of Culture and Arts.

in 1981. Since then, the annual event has attracted hundreds of artists, musicians, and performers as well as tens of thousands of visitors. Noor valued the event not only because it showcased the region's culture, but because it brought attention to the area's rich architecture. Initially, the event met with some criticism as people suggested that it was anti-Arab or anti-Muslim. But eventually, the festival came to be appreciated and respected.

Noor became involved with several other projects related to the arts. The National Music Conservatory was established to help up-and-coming musicians by teaching them classical Arabic and Western music, encouraging music appreciation, and promoting the training of music teachers. The queen also created the National Handicrafts Development Project. This program encouraged Jordanians—especially the women—to take pride in their handmade crafts and clothing. In addition to promoting the culture of Jordan, the project helped teach the craftspeople how to make a living by selling their works.

In 1984, Queen Noor began working on a new project, the creation of the Jubilee School. Opened in 1993, it is an independent, coeducational school for gifted children who come from various cultural and economic backgrounds. Her idea was to bring a diverse group of children together and teach them about community service. She explained:

> *We do not want simply to produce edu-cated young people, important as that is; we hope to nurture educated activists and future leaders who can identify and help to resolve the challenges within their own societies and contribute to stability, peace and justice in the wider world.*

61

Queen Noor sits among graduates of Jubilee School's class of 2000.

Many underprivileged children attend the school on scholarship. Today, Jubilee graduates often rank in the top 10 percent of graduates in Jordan. And 99 percent attend well-respected colleges throughout the world.

In spite of such successes, however, there were still times when Queen Noor struggled to be accepted by the people of Jordan. At one point in 1989, while the king and queen were in Washington, D.C., riots broke out in the streets of Jordan. Citizens were protesting the high cost of fuel, water, and telephone and electrical services. Much to Noor's dismay, some of the health clinics she supported were damaged in the violence. Upon their return to Jordan, the king put an end to the riots by imposing martial law, and he passed government reforms that helped satisfy the people.

Nevertheless, there was another casualty of these riots: Queen Noor's reputation. Somehow rumors began that the queen spent money irresponsibly and didn't care about the financial strains her people endured. She supposedly bought a ring for $5,000, but as people continued to complain and gossip, the story changed to the ring being worth $1 million, and finally to her buying an entire jewelry collection for $20 million. Someone even circulated a fake copy of a check she had written for the purchase.

These rumors filled the queen with anxiety, and she worried about how the people would react to her when she visited villagers for the first time following the riots:

> *I drove myself in my Jeep, as I always did. Hundreds of people rushed out to the road to greet me, waving and calling my name. When I arrived at the village, it was if nothing had happened. Looking at the crowd of welcoming faces, I felt that the weight of the world had been lifted from my shoulders. As they always do, the rumors subsided as it became apparent that they had no substance.* ❧

8 A TIME OF WAR

ⲉⳉⲭⳉⲟ

In 1989, Queen Noor visited Iraq, a neighboring country to Jordan. While there, she was alarmed when she saw schoolchildren being taught to worship the Iraqi leader Saddam Hussein. He seemed to rule over his people in a frightening way. She worried that his leadership was not a healthy one. He had long been battling Iran, a country on the Iraqi border. He accused Iran's leaders of trying to force the Iranian form of religion on Iraq. Saddam also began to complain about Kuwait, a country east of Jordan. He claimed that this nation was engaging in illegal oil-drilling practices and even stealing oil from Iraqi land.

The production of oil in the Middle East is very important to the region, as well as to the Western

Queen Noor was escorted by members of the military on her way to visit refugees who were displaced when Iraq invaded Kuwait.

From 1979 until 2003, Saddam Hussein—who is no relation to King Hussein—was the dictator of Iraq. He had a reputation as a violent and unfair ruler. There are reports that he killed thousands of his own people while he was in power. He led his country in a war against Iran (1980–1988) as well as an invasion of Kuwait in 1990. When the United States drove the Iraqis out of Kuwait in 1991, Saddam remained in power. But after the United States invaded Iraq in March 2003, Saddam fled the Iraqi capital. In December 2003, Saddam was discovered hiding underground in the town of Tikrit. He was charged with war crimes and crimes against humanity.

nations that purchase the oil. When the oil supply is threatened, the whole world takes notice. So after Iraq invaded Kuwait in 1990, many countries, including the United States, got involved. King Hussein wanted a peaceful solution and urged world leaders to negotiate with Saddam Hussein. But such an idea was rejected, and King Hussein was left out of the discussions about Iraq. The newly elected U.S. President George H.W. Bush quickly began to gather support for driving Iraq out of Kuwait.

The situation was very discouraging for King Hussein. There were times when he even considered giving up his title. The United States and other nations did not understand why the king was trying so hard to keep peace. What they couldn't see was how difficult a war against Iraq would be for Jordan. When Iraq invaded Kuwait, Kuwaiti citizens began fleeing into Jordan. In fact, 10,000 refugees arrived each day, and by the end of the conflict, the small nation of 3.5 million people had taken in another 3 million refugees. The unemployment rate rose to 30 percent. And the value of the Jordan currency, the dinar, began to fall. The nation's economy was not strong enough to handle all the new people. At first, even basic supplies, like blankets or tents, were in short supply. If Iraq was under attack, its people would seek refuge in Jordan as well.

As the Kuwaiti people came to Jordan, Queen Noor spent a great deal of time at the border. She tried to help the refugees and arrange for transportation for those who needed it. She reached out to others for help, including British entrepreneur Richard Branson of Virgin Atlantic Airways, who quickly flew

Queen Noor visited refugees at the border between Iraq and Jordan both before and during the war.

in supplies and offered further support. Foreigners like Branson were not the only ones to extend aid to refugees. Noor was touched by the generosity of the Jordanians who provided shelter, food, and supplies like blankets to those who needed it. "Even the poor people in the country were giving more than they could afford. It was an extraordinary moment of grace for the people of Jordan," she said.

In the meantime, Noor had long talks with her husband, assuring him that his place was as king and that the people of Jordan needed him. She convinced him to visit the United States and speak with President Bush in person. He agreed, but Bush did not agree with the king's ideas about negotiation, and the meeting was unsuccessful. To make matters worse, some leaders, such as Egypt's Hosni Mubarak, accused King Hussein of taking bribes from Iraq and of supporting the Iraqi invasion of Kuwait. Mubarak spread these rumors to the United States as well as to other Arab nations. The king defended himself as best he could, but it was hard to counter these accusations. Saudi Arabia, fearing that Jordan was not to be trusted, forced Jordan's diplomats out of their country and cut off the oil supply to Jordan.

Queen Noor knew that she had to speak out in defense of her husband. At a conference at the United Nations, she confronted Suzanne Mubarak, the Egyptian president's wife, who was once her

Map shows boundaries of 1991.

friend. She told Suzanne that her husband's lies were unfair and unfounded. At the same event, she also spoke with President and Mrs. Bush, trying to explain how serious the refugee situation in Jordan had become. But the Bushes still believed that military action was the only answer. First lady Barbara Bush later described Noor as being a traitor to the United States, her native country. Further, some reporters

Iraq stood to gain better access to the Persian Gulf if it controlled Kuwait.

claimed that King Hussein was a coward who needed his wife to speak for him.

Meanwhile, Saddam Hussein had been given a deadline of January 15, 1991, to withdraw Iraqi troops from Kuwait. If he did not do so by that date, he would have to face military forces from around the world. King Hussein met with Saddam and tried to convince him to leave Kuwait. The king said, "If you do not make the decision on your own to get out of Kuwait, you are going to be driven out. The whole world is against you." But Saddam would not change his position.

As the threat of war grew closer, Queen Noor took the four youngest children to Austria to stay with her sister, Alexa Halaby, during their winter break. They were only 10, 8, 7, and 4—too young, Noor believed, to be in Jordan when violence erupted. She stayed in Austria for a bit, spending as much time with them as she could. She later wrote, "The simple act of reading them a bedtime story reduced me to tears. I tried not to focus on our parting, but it was impossible." She made arrangements with her sister about caring for the children in case she and the king did not survive. And then she returned to Jordan to stand by her husband and her people.

The Persian Gulf War, as it came to be known, began in January 1991 as international forces launched an air campaign on Baghdad, the Iraqi

A pro-Iraq demonstration took place in Amman, Jordan, in January 1991.

capital. Refugees poured into Jordan, and Noor worked hard to help them. The people of Jordan grew angrier at the United States for leading the war on Iraq. Queen Noor tried to balance her feelings toward Jordan, her chosen home, and the United States, where she had been raised.

At the end of their winter recess, the four youngest children returned to Jordan. Though the violence continued, they were happy to be reunited with their parents. Hussein's two oldest sons, Abdullah and Feisal, were officers in the military, and they were called into active duty.

Warplanes bombed roads leading into Jordan and destroyed trucks that were legally carrying oil into the country. The senseless loss of lives grew with each passing day, and the oil shortage became a huge problem. The king realized how angry and frustrated the Jordanians were. In a speech, he protested the attack on the Iraqi people and called once again for negotiations to end the violence. He asked, "Which voices will win in the end? The voices of reason, peace, and justice, or the voices of war, hatred, and insanity?"

These words instantly helped the situation in Jordan. Morale improved, and suddenly the once-angry people of Jordan had more respect for and trust in King Hussein. They finally understood that the king was on their side. Some say the king saved his own life by giving that speech. However, the Western nations, including the United States, were furious. They saw the king's comments as critical of the war and supportive of Saddam Hussein. He tried to explain that he was concerned for the people of Iraq, not necessarily for its leader. But his explanations fell on deaf ears.

Meanwhile, incredible rumors about the king and queen spread. Noor remembered:

> In the second month of the conflict, the
> [Washington] Post reported—and other
> publications around the world picked up
> the story—that I had visited Palm Beach,
> Florida, in the midst of the crisis and
> had acquired a seven-acre estate (there
> was even a picture of it) for my husband

and me when we fled Jordan. The reports had us refurbishing a house in Vienna in grand style as our exile-in-waiting. Jordan, they all concluded, was doomed.

But in reality, the king and queen had no intention of leaving, no matter what happened. Although they were ready to fight against the slanderous reports, the rumors began to take a toll on them. "So many fires to put out," Noor wrote in her journal. "I despair of Hussein's depressed spirit. It is becoming more and more difficult to see light at the end of the tunnel."

Just six weeks later, in March 1991, the Gulf War ended and Iraq was defeated by the international forces. Saddam Hussein survived the war, but harsh sanctions were imposed on his country, making it nearly impossible for Iraq to trade with other nations. This hurt Jordan because Iraq was its largest trading partner. Jordan also suffered as hundreds of thousands of people from Kuwait and Saudi Arabia entered the small country, quickly increasing its population by 15 percent. Schools were overcrowded again. And the immunization programs that Queen Noor had worked so hard to create

Around 400,000 people of Jordanian descent returned to Jordan after being forced to leave Kuwait and Saudi Arabia. Among these people was the Al Yasin family from Kuwait. Their daughter Rania became part of the royal family when she married King Hussein's oldest son, Prince Abdullah in 1993.

suddenly couldn't keep up with the demand. There was even an outbreak of polio in some areas.

Throughout the world, many countries were still angry with Jordan for remaining neutral during the conflict. One newspaper reported that Jordan had provided military supplies to Iraq during the war. This allegation was not true, and the paper eventually printed a correction. But the damage had been done.

Queen Noor tried to help her country by building the tourism industry. She met with European tour operators and writers and told them all about the wonders of Jordan. Before long, people from all over the globe traveled to Jordan to visit its beautiful sites. And exhibits of Jordanian treasures were sent to museums in other countries. Little by little, the anger some nations felt toward Jordan and King Hussein began to ease.

But the relationship between Noor and Hussein was suffering. The Gulf War had been a difficult time, and both the king and queen felt its pressure. To make matters worse, rumors spread that King Hussein was involved with another woman. Initially, Queen Noor ignored the rumors, but they persisted. Soon she heard that the king planned to divorce her and marry someone else. Noor began to think about what her life would be like if she and the king ended their marriage. It saddened her to consider how her children would feel, but she convinced herself that she would survive, one way or the other. Before she gave up on her marriage, however, she confronted her husband. He was shocked and surprised by the rumors that had been spread. He assured her that they were not true. Ultimately, Noor believed him and trusted that Hussein had remained faithful to her. Nonetheless, the rumors continued, and the king and queen had to withstand all that was being said.

But in August 1992, the couple forgot about the rumors and instead had to face questions about King Hussein's health. An unusual growth had been found in his body, and at first doctors suspected cancer. The king underwent surgery in the United States at the Mayo Clinic in Minnesota. Precancerous cells were removed, and doctors believed that the king had no further reason to worry. This health scare was difficult for the king and queen to endure. Yet it brought them closer together. Noor remembered:

> *I had never seen him so weak and vulnerable. ... The bond of trust between us strengthened. Both of us had been so busy and preoccupied with our work over the past difficult years, but in the hospital he had every reassurance that he, and he alone, was my number-one priority.*

The king gained a new enthusiasm for life, and he appreciated his wife more than ever. ❧

9 CARING FOR THE KING

❧⟨×⟩☙

When news of King Hussein's surgery got out, leaders from around the world were concerned. President and Mrs. Bush invited the king and queen to the White House for dinner. It seemed as though the negative feelings they all had previously felt just disappeared. When the couple returned to Jordan, people gathered in the streets to welcome them home.

As Hussein returned to work, his hope for peace in the Middle East was stronger than ever. But the tensions between Israel and the Palestinians never seemed to end. With the support of U.S. President Bill Clinton, who had been elected in 1992, both parties had signed a peace treaty, called the Oslo Accords, at the White House. King Hussein was saddened that Jordan had not been consulted or

Yitzhak Rabin was born in Jerusalem in 1922. As a young man, he served in a commando unit of the Jewish community, and in the Israeli army. He was the chief of staff of Israel's armed forces during the Six-Day War in 1967. In 1968, he was appointed Israeli ambassador to the United States. He returned to Israel in 1973 and became involved in politics. The following year, he became prime minister. He lost his bid for reelection in 1977, but he became prime minister again in 1992.

included. But in the years to come, he met with Prime Minister Yitzhak Rabin of Israel. The two leaders began work on their own peace treaty, and their talks were very encouraging. Before long, President Clinton wanted to be part of the process. He asked that the signing of the declaration of peace be in Washington, D.C., instead of Jordan. At first, the king thought that idea was ridiculous. But when the United States offered to forgive the $700 million debt that Jordan owed, the king changed his mind. He hated to make such a decision based on only money, but he knew what was best for his country.

The negotiations between Israel and Jordan were not always easy, but in the end, the two leaders were successful. In July 1994, King Hussein and Prime Minister Rabin met on the White House lawn and signed the Washington Declaration. This document ended 46 years of conflict between the two nations. It stated that Jordan and Israel would share electricity grids to conserve energy, their borders would open, and their airspace would

U.S. President Bill Clinton watches as King Hussein and Prime Minister Rabin sign the Washington Declaration.

be available to each other.

After signing the document, both leaders addressed a joint session of Congress, and their speeches were well-received. As Noor later wrote, "After the signing, our image changed virtually overnight, it seemed, and suddenly ... we could do no wrong." Once back in Jordan, she found that the Jordanians were supportive and cautiously enthusiastic about the new agreement. The following October, the official Jordanian-Israeli Peace Treaty was signed in Jordan.

The following year, Queen Noor was attending an event in Swaziland when she received terrible news. Prime Minister Rabin had been shot and killed. His death was a terrible blow to her and her husband, as well as to people throughout the world. He was killed by an extremist from his own country. King Hussein and Queen Noor traveled to Jerusalem for his funeral, and they expressed their sadness to his widow, Leah.

The loss of Rabin meant that the king and queen would need to work even harder to promote harmony in the Middle East. The new prime minister of Israel was Benjamin Netanyahu. His views were in sharp contrast to those of the Jordanian king and queen, and he had very little patience for the PLO and its views.

Queen Noor channeled her energy into many projects, including the United World Colleges, an organization of schools that encourages under-standing and tolerance of all people, and Seeds of Peace, a program that unites Israeli and Palestinian children. But as she worked for peace, more trouble was on the horizon. The king's health began to get worse.

King Hussein suffered from fevers, and he lacked energy. In 1998, he returned to the Mayo Clinic and was informed that he had non-Hodgkin's lymphoma, a type of cancer, and that it had spread throughout his body. Noor was filled with worry:

> *I felt such fear, such bottomless anxiety at the thought of losing my husband, my best friend, my dearest love and inspira-tion that it threatened to paralyze me. For twenty years we had been husband and wife, father and mother, life partners*

*through international crises and domestic
turmoil in Jordan. ... To lose this man
would be a catastrophe on every level
imaginable. He simply could not die.*

King Hussein stayed at the hospital for treatment,
including chemotherapy, and Queen Noor seldom
left his side. In between treatments, the king and
queen spent time at River House, their 10-acre estate
on the Potomac just outside Washington, D.C. The
home had been purchased in the 1980s when the
couple required more security than a hotel could
provide during their stays in the United States.

While they were at River House, they were
invited to casual dinners at the White House, hosted
by President and Mrs. Clinton. The queen also talked
to the Clintons about the problem of land mines that

*Queen Noor
worked to rid
Bosnia, a coun-
try in south-
eastern Europe,
of its land
mines.*

According to the International Campaign to Ban Landmines, the Ottawa Mine Ban Treaty is "the most comprehensive international instrument for ridding the world of the scourge of mines." The treaty addresses the use of mines, their production and trade, clearance of mines, and destruction of stockpiles. It also provides guidelines for assisting people who have been the victims of mines. As of January 2005, 144 countries have ratified the treaty. This means they have agreed to follow its directions. But many important countries have not signed the treaty, including China, Egypt, Finland, India, Israel, Russia, and the United States.

still exist throughout the world. The highly explosive devices were buried underground during times of war, but they remain active and are now a threat to the people who live near them. Having had visited countries that have been ravaged by land mines, Noor made it a personal mission to encourage world leaders to sign the Ottawa Mine Ban Treaty, a treaty designed to ban the use of land mines throughout the world. The Clintons expressed their support for disarming the mines, but the United States did not officially support the treaty. In the years since, the disarming of land mines has continued to be an important cause for the queen.

While he was in the hospital, King Hussein tried to work as much as he could. He read magazines and newspapers, keeping himself informed about all that was happening in the world. In 1998, President Clinton planned to meet with Prime Minister Benjamin Netanyahu of Israel and the PLO's Yasser Arafat at the Wye Summit

Accords in Maryland. Negotiations between the two
men were hindered by repeated instances of violence
in the Middle East.

King Hussein strongly supported Clinton's
efforts, so he flew to Maryland to help. Queen Noor
accompanied him, watching to make sure he did not
exhaust himself. King Hussein spoke to Netanyahu
and Arafat, urging them to be reasonable, to think
of the future of their countries. In the end, his words

*King Hussein
and President
Clinton watch
as PLO leader
Arafat (left)
shakes hands
with Israeli
Prime Minister
Netanyahu at
the Wye Summit
Accords.*

were successful, and both men agreed to the Wye Memorandum. A determined but weak Hussein attended the official signing at the White House on October 23, 1998.

Leaders from around the world were stunned to see how frail the king looked at that October signing. But the following month, King Hussein appeared on television and announced to the people of Jordan that he had beaten the disease and was cancer-free. After five and a half months at the Mayo Clinic, the king and queen were finally cleared to leave. Although the king's medical reports were favorable, Noor continued to worry about her husband's health.

They spent some time recovering at the River House and then went on to England. When the royal couple returned to Jordan in January 1999, they did so on a Gulfstream 4 aircraft, with Hussein in the pilot's seat. First, after leaving England, a British Royal Air Force fighter accompanied them. As they continued into France, a French fighter plane took over the escort. This continued with Italian and Israeli fighters as they

King Hussein announced the positive results of his tests in a television interview on November 13, 1998: "Chemotherapy is over and, thank God, there is no trace of the lymphoma. ... Although stages of treatment were quite hard and difficult, they were nothing compared to one's morale. Thank God that everything is proceeding in a good manner. By God's will, this will be the final stage after which I will return home."

King Hussein knelt down and prayed when he finally reached Jordan after months of cancer treatment at the Mayo Clinic.

passed through Europe and into the Middle East. The international gesture was a moving tribute to the king, who worked so hard for peace throughout the world. Finally, a Jordanian aircraft finished the escort as the tired king and queen came home. ॐ

10 ON HER OWN

Chapter

ෙ૭ઝ૭ૐ

Once the royal couple was back in Jordan, the king realized that he needed to think about his successor. His brother Hassan could be named as next in line, but the Jordanian people were not that fond of him and there were rumors that he disliked Queen Noor. So King Hussein instead looked to his oldest son, Abdullah, whose mother was the king's second wife. Some thought that Queen Noor had wished her older son, Hamzah, would be named. But she says she was actually pleased that he would have time to grow up and graduate from college, before taking on the responsibility of serving the public. Queen Noor completely supported Abdullah and his wife, Rania, to take over the throne when the time came.

That time was soon to come. Shortly after his

Queen Noor received an honorary doctorate degree from Brown University in 1999. The late King Hussein was also honored with a degree from the university.

King Abdullah II was born on January 30, 1962. He is the oldest son of King Hussein and Princess Muna, the king's second wife. King Abdullah II is an accomplished pilot and parachutist, and he served in the Jordanian military, eventually being promoted to major general. As king, he is trying to continue his father's legacy by keeping Jordan strong and promoting peace in the Middle East.

decision about Abdullah, King Hussein discovered his cancer had returned. He and Noor flew back to the Mayo Clinic, and more rounds of chemotherapy began. But the king did not improve. Doctors warned Noor that his condition was very serious. When it became clear that the king would not recover, Noor made an important decision. She took her husband home. It was her belief that he should not spend his final hours in a U.S. hospital, but rather in his own country, surrounded by his family and friends. Back in Amman, the king was cared for in the medical center that now bears his name. And on February 7, 1999, with Queen Noor holding his hand, King Hussein breathed his final breath.

The queen had suffered a terrible loss, but she knew she needed to be strong for her children as well as for the people of Jordan. The king's body was brought back to the palace and the casket was placed in the drawing room. That night, Noor slept in the room with a single candle burning under a portrait of her husband. She remembers, "I was in shock, yes, but I was also imbued with an extraordinary feeling

Queen Noor and daughters Raiyah and Iman receive condolences following King Hussein's death.

of peace. Words cannot adequately express the serenity and simple faith that sustained me at that time, convinced as I was that this was just another phase of the journey that we would continue to travel together." She later came to realize that she "would never fear death but see it as a chance for reunion."

According to Muslim tradition, funerals are attended only by men. But Queen Noor broke that tradition and was present at the king's funeral. Her actions were reminiscent of her bold decision to attend her own wedding more than 20 years before. Leaders from around the world came to the funeral to pay respect to the man who had fought for peace for so long. Among them were Prime Minister Benjamin Netanyahu of Israel, President Hosni Mubarak of Egypt, Prince Charles from England, and U.N. Secretary General Kofi Annan. Also in attendance were three former U.S. presidents—Gerald Ford, George H.W. Bush, and Jimmy Carter—as well as President Bill Clinton, who had thoughtfully brought Queen Noor's parents with him on Air Force One. The people of Jordan mourned the loss of their courageous king.

After the king's death, Noor kept her title of queen, but she shares it with Queen Rania. Since some of her children are still in school on the East Coast of the United States, Noor has relocated to the Washington, D.C., area. But she still feels a strong connection to Jordan and visits the country once a month or so.

In recent years, Queen Noor has become even more of a celebrity.

When Rania married Abdullah on June 10, 1993, she did not expect to be queen. Her husband was not the natural successor to the throne, until King Hussein named him in 1999. She and her husband have four children—two sons and two daughters—and she works hard to improve the lives of her people. Queen Rania is especially interested in developing income-producing projects, bringing information technology to Jordan's schools, and protecting children from violence.

Noor at a book signing in France for her memoir.

When *Leap of Faith*, her best-selling memoir, was published in 2003, thousands of people lined up at her book signings. She is a popular speaker and in 2005 made $60,000 for each speech she gave on the lecture circuit. She attends elite events such as the Kennedy Center Honors in Washington and the National Symphony Ball. But she is still fairly shy and doesn't enjoy small talk. Real issues interest her, not idle chat.

Noor holds a position with the International Campaign to Ban Landmines and works with the Landmine Survivors Network. She also serves on a number of boards and committees throughout the world. She is an ambassador for Future Harvest, a group of research centers that strives to solve agriculture problems. She is a trustee of the American Cancer Society Foundation, a member of the International Commission on Peace and Food, and president of the United World Colleges. She is a patron of the World Conservation Union, honorary president of BirdLife International, and a board member of the World Wildlife Fund International.

As the years have passed, Noor continues to speak out about issues that are important to her. Some of her comments have drawn criticism, but she does not let that deter her. For instance, she wrote very openly in *Leap of Faith*, and some people felt she had said too much about politics. After the United States led another invasion of Iraq in 2003, Noor expressed concern for the Iraqi people. Her words angered many Americans, who felt she was attacking

the policies of the United States. Noor dismissed such ideas and instead tried to help. She spoke out against the Muslim extremists who believe that killing innocent people of the West—by beheadings and suicide bombings—is justified by their religion. She urged Muslims to stand up to the extremists, who she believes are harming the reputation of Islam.

As both a child of the United States and a queen

Queen Noor's work continues to place her alongside world leaders like Nelson Mandela.

93

Although no longer a ruling queen, Noor continues to share her views on world issues.

of an Arab nation, Noor can often see both sides of world issues. In an interview with CBC News of Canada, Queen Noor once spoke about the world's perception of Islam. She explained that Muslim extremists do not fairly represent their religion. She also said that the terrorist activity on September 11, 2001, "was an absolute distortion of Islam and its teachings ... And the majority of Muslims and the

Arab world were horrified by what happened on that day. They took it personally that their own faith and cultural values were being hijacked, but also they felt ... empathy and compassion and great sadness at the loss of life."

On November 9, 2005, Jordan faced terrorism within its borders when suicide bombers killed nearly 60 people at three hotels in Amman. Once again, Noor spoke out. In an interview with CNN she said she believed extremist groups would lose support following the attack. "I personally think they've made a significant tactical error here, because they have attacked innocent civilians, primarily Muslims."

Whether as Lisa Halaby or as Queen Noor, she has always tried to be herself, to remain true to her own feelings, and still consider the people she affects. At her home in McLean, Virginia, she explained to a *Washington Post* reporter in 2004, "I have been trying, and I admit very awkwardly, to try to strike a balance where I can live a normal, natural life here, where I don't do anything here or in Jordan that I would not be comfortable with in either place." And that is no small task. But no matter what the challenge, Queen Noor has never stopped working for the rights of people of all backgrounds. Peace and justice have been, and will continue to be, her goals for nations throughout the world. ℘

NOOR'S LIFE

1969

Enters Princeton University as a member of its first coeducational class

1951

Lisa Najeeb Halaby is born on August 23 in Washington, D.C.

1971

Takes time off from college and travels to Aspen, Colorado, where she works as a waitress and maid, as well as at the Aspen Institute

1970

1966

The National Organization for Women (NOW) is established to work for equality between women and men

1951

Libya gains its independence with help from the United Nations

1971

The first microprocessor is produced by Intel

WORLD EVENTS

1976

Visits Jordan for the first time; meets King Hussein on a later trip

1975

Accepts a position with Llewelyn-Davis and moves to Iran

1974

Graduates from Princeton with a degree in architecture and urban planning and takes a job in Australia

1975

1974

Scientists find that chlorofluorocarbons— chemicals in coolants and propellants—are damaging Earth's ozone layer

1976

U.S. military academies admit women

NOOR'S LIFE

1978

Marries King
Hussein on
June 15

1979

Establishes the
Royal Endowment
for Culture and
Education; chairs the
National Committee
for the Child

1980

Gives birth to
Prince Hamzah on
March 29; visits the
United States for
the first time since
becoming queen

1978

The first test-tube
baby conceived
outside its mother's
womb is born in
Oldham, England

1979

The Soviet Union
invades Afghanistan

1980

The United States
boycotts the Olympic
Games in Moscow
in protest of the
Soviet invasion
of Afghanistan

WORLD EVENTS

1981

Gives birth to Prince Hashim on June 10; begins the Jerash Festival of Culture and Arts

1983

Gives birth to Princess Iman on April 24

1986

Gives birth to Princess Raiyah on February 9

1985

1981

Sandra Day O'Connor becomes the first woman on the U.S. Supreme Court

1983

The AIDS (acquired immune deficiency syndrome) virus is identified

1986

The U.S. space shuttle *Challenger* explodes, killing all seven astronauts on board

NOOR'S LIFE

1990

Works in refugee camps after Iraq invades Kuwait

1991

With her husband, tries to prevent the Gulf War; confronts her husband about rumors of a romantic affair

1992

Goes with King Hussein to the Mayo Clinic in Rochester, Minnesota, where he undergoes an operation

1990

1990

Political prisoner Nelson Mandela, a leader of the anti-apartheid movement in South Africa, is released; Mandela becomes president of South Africa in 1994

1991

The Soviet Union collapses and is replaced by the Commonwealth of Independent States

1994

Genocide of 500,000 to 1 million of the minority Tutsi group by rival Hutu people in Rwanda

WORLD EVENTS

2003

Publishes *Leap of Faith*, her autobiography

1999

Stays by King Hussein's side as he dies; breaks Muslim tradition by attending his funeral

2005

Speaks out against worst terrorist attack in Jordan's history, which kills nearly 60 people

2005

1996

A sheep is cloned in Scotland

2000

Draft of the human genome is completed

2005

Major earthquake kills thousands in Pakistan

FULL NAME: Queen Noor Al Hussein

BIRTH NAME: Lisa Najeeb Halaby

DATE OF BIRTH: August 23, 1951

BIRTHPLACE: Washington, D.C.

FATHER: Najeeb Elias Halaby
(1915–2003)

MOTHER: Doris Carlquist Halaby

EDUCATION: Princeton University

SPOUSE: King Hussein bin Talal
(1935–1999)

DATE OF MARRIAGE: June 15, 1978

CHILDREN: Hamzah (1980–)
Hashim (1981–)
Iman (1983–)
Raiyah (1986–)

FURTHER READING

Darraj, Susan Muaddi. *Queen Noor*. Philadelphia: Chelsea House, 2003.

Harris, Nathaniel. *Israel and the Arab Nations in Conflict*. Austin: Raintree, 1999.

Skinner, Patricia. *Jordan*. Milwaukee: Gareth Stevens, 2003.

South, Coleman. *Jordan*. New York: Benchmark Books, 1997

Wagner, Heather Lehr. *King Abdullah II*. Philadelphia: Chelsea House, 2005.

LOOK FOR MORE SIGNATURE LIVES BOOKS ABOUT THIS ERA:

Benazir Bhutto: *Pakistani Prime Minister and Activist*
ISBN 0-7565-1578-5

Fidel Castro: *Leader of Communist Cuba*
ISBN 0-7565-1580-7

Winston Churchill: *British Soldier, Writer, Statesman*
ISBN 0-7565-1582-3

Jane Goodall: *Legendary Primatologist*
ISBN 0-7565-1590-4

Adolf Hitler: *Dictator of Nazi Germany*
ISBN 0-7565-1589-0

Eva Perón: *First Lady of Argentina*
ISBN 0-7565-1585-8

Joseph Stalin: *Dictator of the Soviet Union*
ISBN 0-7565-1597-1

On the Web

For more information on *Queen Noor*, use FactHound.

1. Go to *www.facthound.com*
2. Type in a search word related to this book or this book ID: 0756515955
3. Click on the *Fetch It* button.

FactHound will find Web sites related to this book.

Historic Sites

Madaba Archaeological Park
Madaba, Jordan
Tel. 08-544056
Inaugurated by Queen Noor, a park containing a collection of Byzantine churches and some of Jordan's most impressive ancient mosaics

The Jordan Design & Trade Center
Shmeisani District
Amman, Jordan
Tel. 06-5699141
Created with Queen Noor's help, a center devoted to developing Jordan's handicraft industry, featuring a retail showroom and handmade items

autonomy
the right to self-government

communism
a social system in which goods and property are
shared in common

established mandates
oversaw the affairs of

extremist
a person whose views or actions are beyond
the norm

guerrilla
a soldier who is not part of a country's
regular army

imbued
completely filled

martial law
control of a people by the government's military,
instead of by civilian forces, often during
an emergency

negotiate
to handle a matter through discussion and
compromise, rather than by force

segregation
the practice of separating people of different races

successor
one who follows, usually in line to a royal or
government position

terrorism
the systematic use of violent or destructive acts as
a way to control other people

Chapter 1

Page 13, line 3: The Hashemite Kingdom of Jordan. Office of Her Majesty Queen Noor. *College of William and Mary Commencement, Virginia.* 11 May 2003. 23 February 2005. www.noor.gov.jo/Speech_Details.asp?SpeechID=175 &CatId=6.

Chapter 2

Page 17, line 3: Queen Noor. *Leap of Faith: Memoirs of an Unexpected Life.* New York: Miramax, 2003, pp. 14–15.

Chapter 3

Page 24, line 27: Ibid., p. 31.

Page 26, line 16: Ibid., p. 33.

Page 29, line 5: Ibid., p. 46

Chapter 4

Page 31, line 10: Ibid., pp. 80–81.

Chapter 6

Page 47, line 14: Susan Muaddi Darraj. *Queen Noor.* Philadelphia: Chelsea House, 2003, p. 55.

Chapter 7

Page 50, line 1: *Leap of Faith: Memoirs of an Unexpected Life*, pp. 163–164.

Page 53, line 6: Ibid., p. 212.

Page 56, line 3: Ibid., p. 218.

Page 56, line 22: Ibid., p. 221.

Page 58, line 20: Ibid., p. 273.

Page 59, line 7: Ibid., p. 210.

Page 61, line 22: The Hashemite Kingdom of Jordan. Office of Her Majesty Queen Noor. *The Jubilee School.* 22 April 2005. www.noor.gov.jo/projects2.htm.

Page 63, line 19: *Leap of Faith: Memoirs of an Unexpected Life*, p. 291.

Chapter 8

Page 68, line 5: Ibid., p. 313.

Page 70, line 8: Ibid., p. 322.

Page 70, line 19: Ibid., p. 325.

Page 72, line 4: Ibid., p. 332.

Page 72, line 22: Ibid., p. 333.

Page 73, line 8: Ibid., p. 333.

Page 75, line 19: Ibid., p. 353.

Chapter 9

Page 79, line 5: Ibid., p. 373.

Page 80, line 23: Ibid., p. 403

Page 82, sidebar: "What is the Mine Ban Treaty?" International Campaign to Ban Landmines. 22 April 2005. www.icbl.org/tools/faq/treaty/what.

Page 84, sidebar: "King Completely Cured from Lymphoma." *Jordan Times* 14 November 1998. 20 September 2005. www.jordanembassyus.org/111498001. htm.

Chapter 10

Page 88, line 27: *Leap of Faith: Memoirs of an Unexpected Life*, p. 433.

Page 89, line 5: Ibid., p. 435.

Page 94, line 7: "An Interview with Queen Noor." *cbc.ca*. Cable News Network. 22 April 2005. www.cbc.ca/sunday/coverstory_queennoor.html.

Page 95, line 11: Brent Sadler, Barbara Starr, and Kristen Gillespie. "Al Qaeda claims four Iraqis behind Amman hotel attacks." *CNN.com* 11 November 2005. 14 November 2005. www.cnn.com/2005/WORLD/meast/11/11/jordan. blasts/index.html.

Page 95, line 19: Roxanne Roberts. "After the Reign: Queen Noor, Bridging Worlds—and Roles—in the Five Years Since Her Husband's Death." *Washington Post* 2 March 2004. 24 February 2005. www.washingtonpost.com/ac2/wp-dyn/A21209-2004Mar1.

"An Interview with Queen Noor." *cbc.ca*. Cable News Network. 22 April 2005. www.cbc.ca/sunday/coverstory_queennoor.html.

"Anwar al-Sadat." Jewish Virtual Library. 3 November 2005. www.jewishvirtuallibrary.org/jsource/biography/sadat.html.

Dallas, Roland. *King Hussein: A Life on the Edge*. New York: Fromm International, 1998.

"Former Pan Am Chief Najeeb Halaby Dies." *Associated Press* 3 July 2003. 22 April 2005. www.dfw.com/mid/kansascity/6224838.htm.

King Abdullah II Official Website – King of the Hashemite Kingdom of Jordan. 3 November 2005. www.kingabdullah.jo.

"Menachim Begin." Jewish Virtual Library. 3 November 2005. www.jewishvirtuallibrary.org/jsource/biography/begin.html.

Official Website of Her Majesty Queen Noor. 23 February 2005. www.noor.gov.jo.

Queen Noor. *Leap of Faith: Memoirs of an Unexpected Life*. New York: Miramax, 2003.

"Queen Noor Reveals Secret of Her Happiness." *Hello* 14 April 2005. 22 April 2005. www.hellomagazine.com/royalty/2005/04/14/queennoor/.

Roberts, Roxanne. "After the Reign: Queen Noor, Bridging Worlds—and Roles—in the Five Years Since Her Husband's Death," *Washington Post* 2 March 2004. 24 February 2005. www.washingtonpost.com/ac2/wp-dyn/A21209-2004Mar1.

Satloff, Michael B. "The Jordan-Israel Peace Treaty: A Remarkable Document." *The Middle East Quarterly* 2.1 (March 1995).

Schneider, Howard. "Queen Noor, Standing Alone: Just Months After King Hussein's Death, His Widow Ponders the Formless Future Her Hands Will Shape," *Washington Post* 19 June 1999. 2 November 2005. www.library.cornell.edu/colldev/mideast/qnoor.htm.

Selskey, Andrew. "AP: Queen Noor Appeals to Muslim Moderates," *ABC News* 25 October 2004. 22 April 2005. www.abcnews.go.com/International/print?id=196652.

"Yasser Arafat." Jewish Virtual Library. 3 November 2005. www.jewishvirtuallibrary.org/jsource/biography/arafat.html.

Lucia Raatma earned a bachelor's degree in English literature from the University of South Carolina and a master's degree in cinema studies from New York University. When she isn't writing books about world leaders, historic battles, or famous athletes, she enjoys going to movies, reading novels, and spending time with her husband and two children. They live in New York.

Image Credits